Sam Gardener

MAX SCHMID

ICELAND
THE EXOTIC NORTH

Iceland Review

ICELAND — THE EXOTIC NORTH
Text: Max Schmid
Photographs: Max Schmid
Design: Gísli B. Björnsson & Fanney Valgardsdóttir
Typesetting: Auglýsingastofan Ltd., Reykjavík
Lithos: Prentmyndastofan Ltd.
Printed in the Netherlands
Iceland Review © 1985, Reykjavík, Iceland

Close look at
a new land

The endless expanses bordering on the Arctic Ocean — those obscure areas at the edge of the atlas page — have long held a special attraction for me, and it was not chance that led me to choose Iceland as my destination in this region. On this island the creative mechanisms of nature have formed a synthesis of contrasting landscapes, which, taken as a whole,

represent something unique on our earth. The rugged part of this scenery may be compared to a rough shell containing hidden natural beauty — the product of the primeval forces of the earth's core, an unfinished process of evolution, and the harsh climate of northern latitudes. The bare and treeless highlands, with their ice-covered mountain chains menacingly

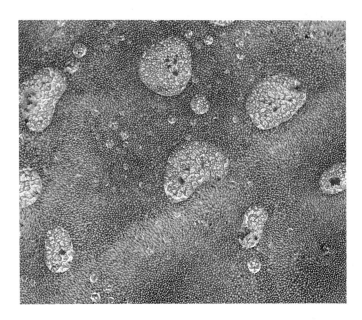

towering over volcanic deserts, are an especially magnificent example of this strange beauty. In spite of their essentially uninviting character, the highlands irresistibly appeal to the explorer in us. Measured against the age of the universe, Iceland has only just been created. If we imagine all of geological time compressed into one 24-hour day, we would have to set the clock back to only 10 minutes before midnight to arrive at the moment of the island's birth. An eventful "day" is almost at an end. Much has happened and receded into the dim past. The dinosaurs, for example, have long since disappeared. But in the short span of time remaining before midnight much will still happen. At the spot where Iceland is about to rise there is only the monotonous surface of the Atlantic. However, tectonic disturbances are in progress and, along the fault line between the Eurasian and North American continental plates, massive recurring basaltic eruptions begin. Soon they become concentrated in the area around what is now Iceland. In a few minutes of our geological day — actually millions of years — the island appears, grows, and then expands further because of the continental drift, reaching its present size of about 103,000 sq km. These processes are by no means over. The face of Iceland, like that of the whole earth, will continue to change, and in the not too distant future the continents will have different outlines. There is reason to believe that these changes, gradual when measured against human notions of time, will occur at a somewhat faster pace in the area around Iceland.

The island is part of the fault system of the Mid-Atlantic Ridge, and of all the regions of that predominantly undersea mountain chain, it has the greatest concentration of volcanoes. On the average, there are rumblings somewhere on the island about every five years, and sometimes events take a serious turn. In 1973, for example, the earth opened in the Westman Islands, and part of the town was covered with volcanic ashes and molten lava. The most catastrophic outburst, however, took place in 1783 when Lakagigar, one of the crater rows typical of Iceland, erupted. Fire spewed from 100 craters simultaneously along the 25-km row, producing the greatest lava flow ever seen by human eyes. Volcanoes slumber even under the great glaciers of the country, such as at Katla and Grímsvötn. They make their presence known from time to time with tremendous eruptions.

On the green outer edges of the island, this volcanic threat is scarcely perceptible; here, the overall impression is determined by the abundance of bird life and the almost luxuriant growth of moss, grass, flowers, and bushes. But anyone venturing into the remote interior parts of Iceland discovers a lifeless world. It is a world nevertheless possessed of a strange beauty all its own: not a chirping bird, not a patch of green, only bizarre mountain formations, naked lava, and black sand. Man, a living creature, has entered a world that knows only dead matter, a world not yet ready to bring forth and sustain life. It is like going back aeons in time to the beginning of the earth's history. An eternal stillness envelops the scorched land, which appears to have just crystallized out of a glowing inferno. Only the wind and the light of the subarctic sun animate the landscape. The lack of vegetation lends an especially primeval atmosphere to the scene, for without the softening cover of plant life the topographical features bring out starkly the existence of nature's mighty landscape-building forces.

The subterranean fire that created all this is still present. Reminders of it may be found in the billowing clouds of steam over geothermal areas anywhere in the country. In general, a distinction is made between two kinds of geothermal activities: hot-water springs and steam vents. The latter, which can develop into mud pots, or solfataras, are found exclusively in high-temperature areas — the youngest volcanic zones. These are directly connected with the furnaces of magma from which hot gases rise. The gases mix with ground water and work their way through labyrinthine passages

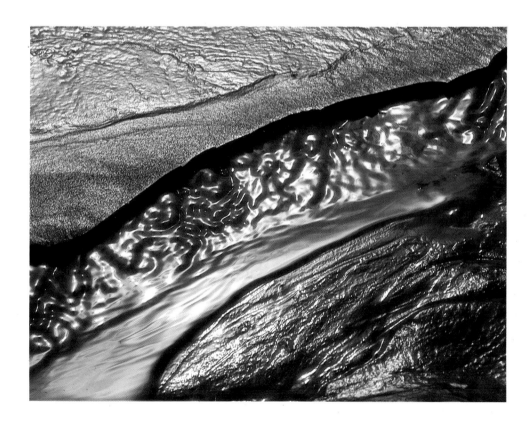

to the surface, creating hissing steam vents and bubbling mud pots where they emerge. The largest area with springs of this kind is near Torfajökull, a glacier in the southern part of the island, and it is among the most outlandish landscapes on the planet. The gently rolling contours of the mountains, light-coloured because of the rhyolite that forms them, make an attractive picture, a kind of "landscape graphics." In the summer, surviving patches of snow draw motley abstract patterns on the sides of mountains notched with valleys, the air filled with the bubbling and hissing of hot springs and the biting smell of sulphur. In this witches' kitchen corrosive gases have eaten away at the stone, exposing all kinds of minerals which here display their magic colours. Even under the glaciers hot springs boil away silently in complete concealment. The heat they give off forms large, grotesque caves inside the ice mass. Thus, nature's ultimate opposites, fire and ice, are united in one place.

Even outside the volcanically active zones the temperature of the earth is often higher than the average, and this is the reason for the numerous hot springs of the sort traditionally associated with Iceland. To this group belong the rare ones that spout hot water and steam – the geysers – often thought of as the hallmark of Iceland. When the right combination of factors exists – a peculiar formation of underground passages through which the water and steam find their way to the surface, special temperature and pressure relationships, and circulatory currents – some of the water deep within the earth is transformed into superheated steam. At regular intervals, the steam forces the rest of the water out of the opening in the earth's surface. The resulting eruption is an impressive sight, indeed, it can also be very amusing to watch the spectators scatter in all directions, too startled to remember taking photographs. In addition to watching a geyser spout, the

In the perspective of geological events, man seems to be a rather meaningless adjunct on a spot of earth dominated by such powerful natural forces. His living space is limited to a narrow coastal strip encircling the island. Here, with unrelenting effort and the aid of the most modern equipment, he cultivates the stony soil. The undemanding sheep deliver wool of the highest quality, and the extensive fishing banks ensure a high standard of living for the country's 230,000 inhabitants. Entire cities are supplied with naturally hot water – a blessing from the danger slumbering under the surface of the earth.

Minor climatic changes or a geological "spasm" can have far-reaching consequences for Iceland. Science continues to look for ways to predict such events so that in the future man will no longer be at their mercy. With growing understanding of these phenomena, the processes of geological transformation appear in a new light of regularity and harmony. Many questions and secrets remain, however, and they are, in fact, part of the fascination of Iceland.

Max Schmid

photographer can use his viewfinder to frame the sinter – the siliceous deposits surrounding the spring's opening – as it creates miniature works of art in the process.

Icelanders seldom speak positively about their climate, which is, however, much milder than might be expected from the country's geographical position. The area around Iceland is a zone where mild oceanic and cold Arctic air masses mix, resulting in changeable and often stormy weather. However, aren't many of the world's most beautiful countries found in regions of high precipitation? The harsh northern climate really acts as a protective shield over the island's untouched landscapes, protecting them from further incursions by civilisation. But in Iceland, too, the sun shines after every storm, and it transforms the idyllic seashore, the luminous glaciers on the horizon, and the green oases in the midst of black deserts into an unreal fairyland.

Heavy precipitation is the decisive factor in the existence of the huge glaciers. About one-ninth of the country lies buried under ice, and in the Vatnajökull, a glacier covering an area of 8,500 sq km, Iceland possesses the largest ice sheet in Europe – thought by some to be a doubtful distinction.

Wild Land, Rough Sea

The coastal landscape is varied, consisting of distinctly different regions. Soft, sandy beaches alternate with stretches of rugged lava cliffs and steep mountains that plunge abruptly into the sea.

Long fjords indent the coast, recalling the activity of ice-age glaciers at the same time as they offer fishermen welcome sheltered harbours. Outside the fjords the northern ocean is constantly heaving, unceasingly wearing away the hardest rock.

Wrecks dot the beaches, rising up accusingly like skeletons. None remain very long; they are soon swallowed again by the sea. Flóki Vilgerdarson, a Norwegian Viking, made an attempt to settle in the Western Fjords in the 9th century. It was there one day that he sighted pack ice and gave the country the name by which it has been known ever since — Iceland.

Beach at Austurhorn, East Iceland.

Látraströnd seen from the island of Hrísey.

White sands add a tropical touch to the beach near Örlygshöfn in Patreksfjördur (right).

The rocks at Cape Dyrhólaey, the
southernmost tip of Iceland.

Display of light and storm clouds over Hvalfjördur.

A formation of columnar basalt defies the onrushing sea near Hofsós in Skagafjördur.

Water Everywhere

Because of heavy precipitation a relatively large number of major rivers, considering the country's total area, drain the interior. Small, cheerfully babbling brooks form a striking contrast to the roaring glacial rivers, which on warm summer days swell to several times their normal volume. The river beds often follow geological rift trenches or plunge over the sides of one of those fractures into deep chasms. Some of the most picturesque and magnificent waterfalls may be found at such spots. Lakes like that at Thingvellir were created by tectonic shifts. Lava flows dammed up the water of Mývatn, whose unique natural setting is one of the wonders of the world.

A brook in Kaldaklofsfjöll reflects a bright
summer day.

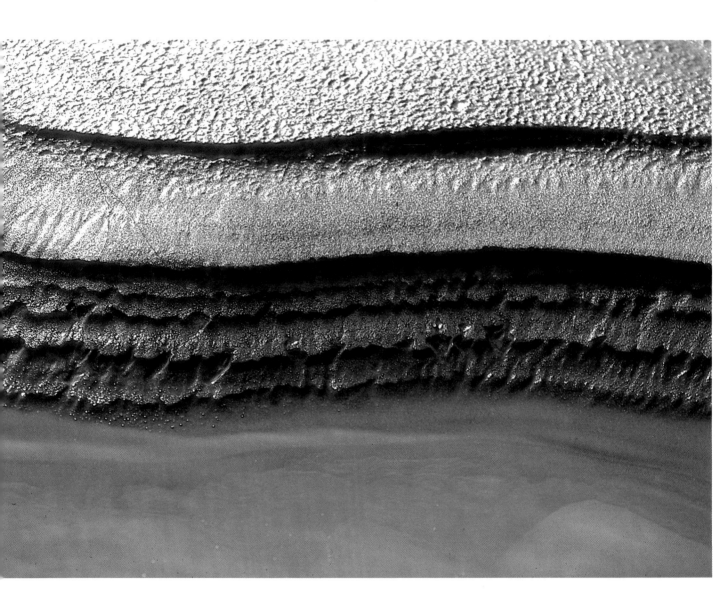

Sand deposits along the shore of a glacial river.

The still waters of Lake Mývatn at midnight.

The midday sun illuminates a mystic corner in Thórsmörk.

Brooks fed by the melt-off from
Langjökull join on the outwash plain below
the glacier.

22

The untamed waters of the river Jökulsá á
Fjöllum roll towards the sea.

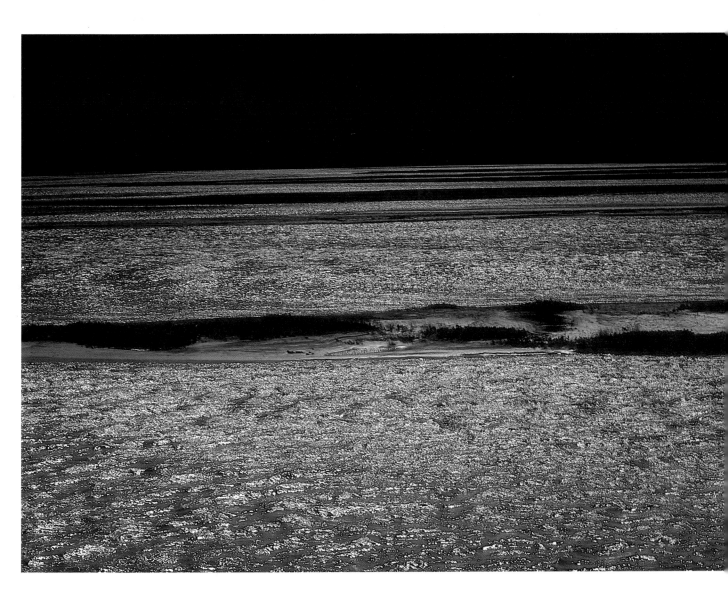

Basalt columns at Svartifoss in the Skaftafell National Park.

Two streams of different temperature join above this nameless waterfall and make it look multicoloured due to algae growth.

The Fight for Life

The absence of trees in Iceland's open spaces is especially striking to foreigners — but only to them. "Trees obstruct the view," people say in Iceland. Has it always looked like this? There are indications that woods existed at the time of the settlement, and looking further back, it is apparent from fossil remains that the island was partly forested at rhythmic intervals. During the time of the medieval commonwealth (930-1262), wood could still be obtained locally, but the worsening of the climate in subsequent centuries hampered regeneration. Today, attempts at afforestation are subject to great difficulties. The ground flora, however, is both beautiful and abundant.

A thick, soft carpet of moss covers the lava field of Eldhraun, partly masking the devastation caused by the eruption of Laki 200 years ago.

Bold autumn colours in a heath landscape at Thingvallavatn.

The so-called fairy ring is formed by the spread of fungi in mossy areas.

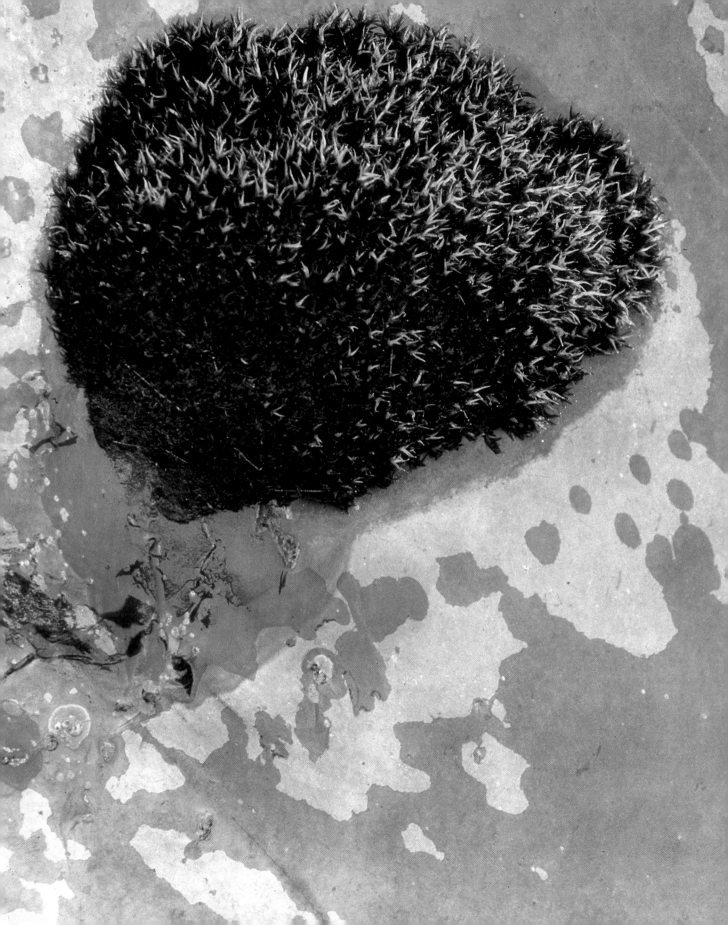

Moss cushion takes hold on the polished surface of an obsidian boulder.

Combed by the wind, cotton grass glows
in the rays of the evening sun.

Floating straws in a pond, blown down by
the wind.

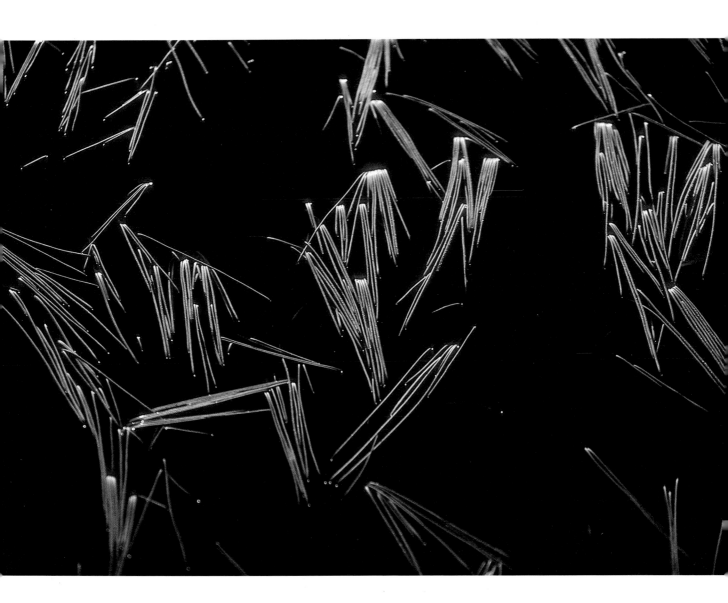

An autumn evening at Thingvallavatn.

Seeds waiting to be borne away by the wind (right).

The Magic of Unearthly Landscape

The highlands were once the playground of elves and trolls and a home for those unenviable human pariahs, the outlaws. Some of the old mystique still adheres to these untouched expanses. The natural phenomena themselves are veiled in mystery and entice the visitor to make exploratory sorties. This corner of the planet has features so different from the normal appearance of earthly continents that it is often compared to the lunar landscape.

When confronted with the mysterious, the human intellect always looks for comparisons with known things, even if it has to look beyond the terrestrial world to do so. Indeed, we must constantly search for words to describe the wonders that our own planet — so rich in contrasts — has brought forth.

A group of pseudocraters near Skútustadir by Mývatn. Craters of this type are formed when lava flows over wetlands.

The bizarre cliffs at Raudhólar by Jökulsá á Fjöllum impress the traveller with their interplay of light, form and colour.

Rhyolite hills add colour to the landscape on Snaefellsnes.

The glow of the yellow rhyolite mountains of Landmannalaugar is intensified by the low sun.

Moss carpets grow lushly in protected slots in front of abstractly-shaped mountain slopes.

A rainy day in a secluded valley of Landmannalaugar.

Bleak, washed-out landscape in the vicinity of Torfajökull.

Gently rolling landscape created by storms and erosion.

Landscape in Reykjafjöll.

The coexistence of plant life, ice and the fire below, at Hrafntinnusker.

Cracks in a mud flat created when mud filled a depression following a volcanic eruption. This area around Leirhnjúkur is one of the most volcanic regions in the country.

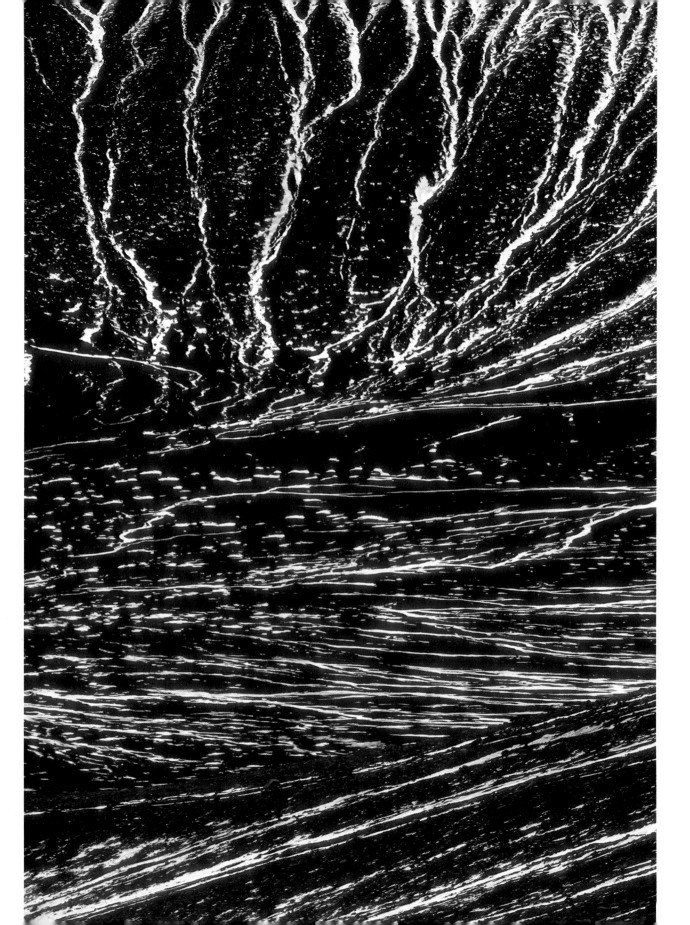

The snow displays "landscape graphics" inside the crater of Hverfjall.

The Hverfjall crater was made by an explosive eruption about 2,500 years ago. In the background the table mountain Búrfell.

The strange landscape near Mývatn
prepares for winter's sleep.

Like a nunatak, a peak in the Kaldaklof mountain range sticks out of a small glacier.

Signs of the Heat Below

The volcanic belt bisects the country diagonally from southwest to northeast. It contains not only all types of volcanoes but also vast geothermal areas. Thousands of individual springs, no two of them identical, gladden the eye with their array of colours and beautiful, filigree-like deposits called sinter.

Hot-spring areas are constantly undergoing transformation. The ground is treacherous, and it wouldn't be surprising if the solfatara valley of Námaskard were one day renamed The Valley of Burned Feet. People should watch their steps here, not only because breaking through the upper crust of the ground may be dangerous, but also out of consideration for the artistically composed patterns of mineral deposits that surround the mouths of the hot springs.

Sulphurous emissions have coloured the
trench winding through the landscape
near Námaskard.

A small mud pot with overflow deposits. Heavy precipitation stimulates solfatara activity and causes many of the bubbling cauldrons to run over.

A solfatara crater in Theistareykir.

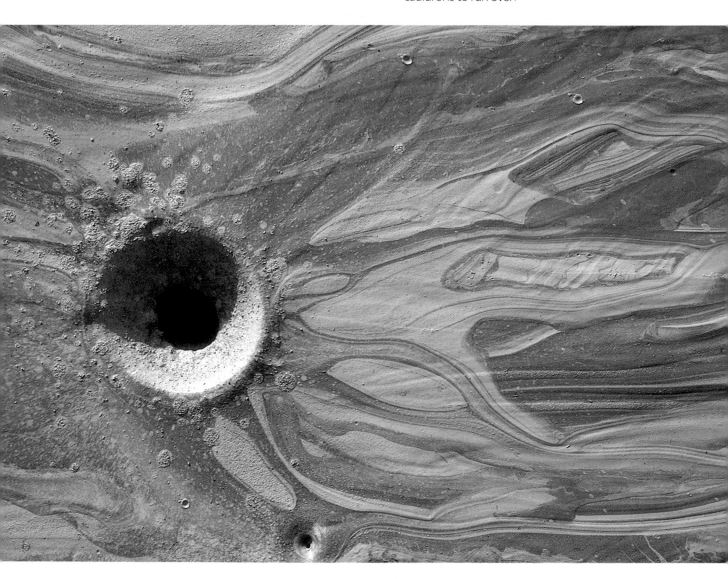

Traces of night frost on muddy sediment
in the vicinity of solfataras.

Transient images of nature on the
solfatara field at Hverarönd.

Algae growth on a rock near a thermal spring.

Sinter terraces at Hveravellir (left).

A solfatara fissure dribbles liquid clay over
the sides of Leirhnjúkur.

Strokkur in action (left).

Mineral deposits surround a hot spring.

A veritable "witches' kitchen" in the area
near Leirhnjúkur, a volcano in an area
seared by the action of subterranean fire.

The fiery eruption of Iceland's most
famous volcano, Hekla, in the summer of
1980, came as a complete surprise.
(See also following pages.)

Hekla on fire. The
column of vapour rose to 15
km high, and lava poured from
a 6-km-long fissure.

The World of Stone

Naked masses of rock characterise the landscape and bear witness to large-scale geological events — literally earth-shaking occurrences. There is hardly a stone here that is not in some way, directly or indirectly, connected with the country's fiery history.

Repeated volcanic eruptions created the basalt strata that are typical of the country, and erosion later chiseled them into remarkable geometrically-shaped mountains. The vast lava fields of Ódádahraun (Lava of Misdeeds), the largest such wasteland on the face of the earth, stem from the more recent past. Lava from some eruptions, such as those of Trölladyngja, a shield volcano, flowed as far as 100 kilometres from its source. Volcanoes of this type produce very thin lava, which solidifies in sheets. Occasionally, basalt may be found which has cooled under special conditions, forming remarkable pillars. Other lava flows piled up during their cooling process to create grotesque ghost cities or black obsidian mountains, whose multi-faceted surfaces reflect the sunlight like cut glass.

The world of stone is in no way dead; it lives in an astounding variety of forms and structures, created under the artistic direction of nature herself, and the open-air museum of that great "abstract artist" is never closed to the visitor.

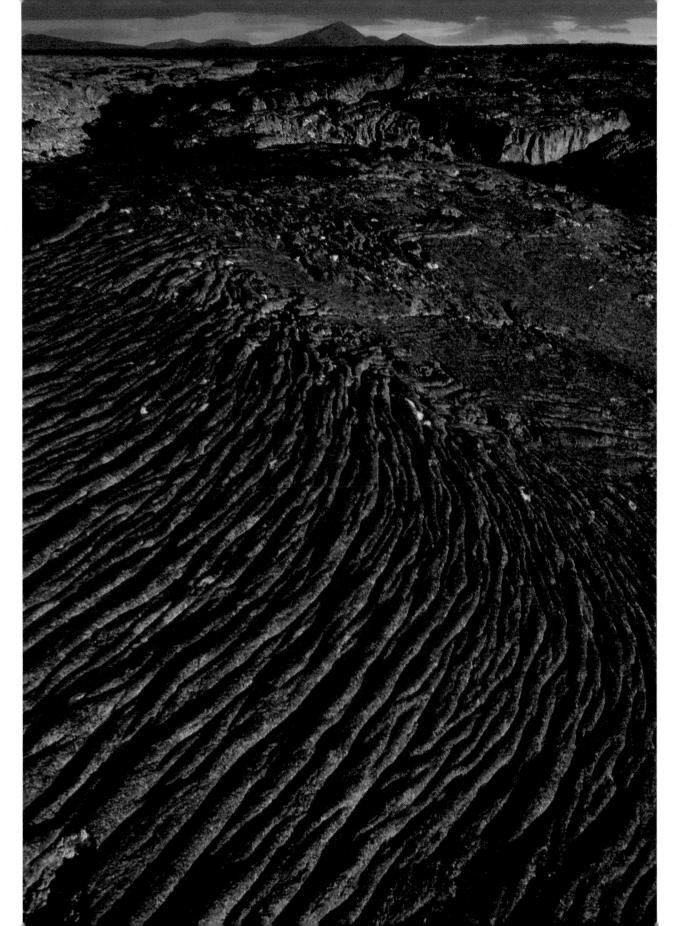

Ropy lava in the desert of Ódáðahraun (preceding page).

Stone strata bent by pressure and heat near Arnarstapi on Snaefellsnes.

Basalt columns near Aldeyjarfoss in northern Iceland.

Nature's architectural triumph. Basalt columns in cross-section at Svartifoss.

There are no limits to nature's creative imagination. Figures in glass-like obsidian lava.

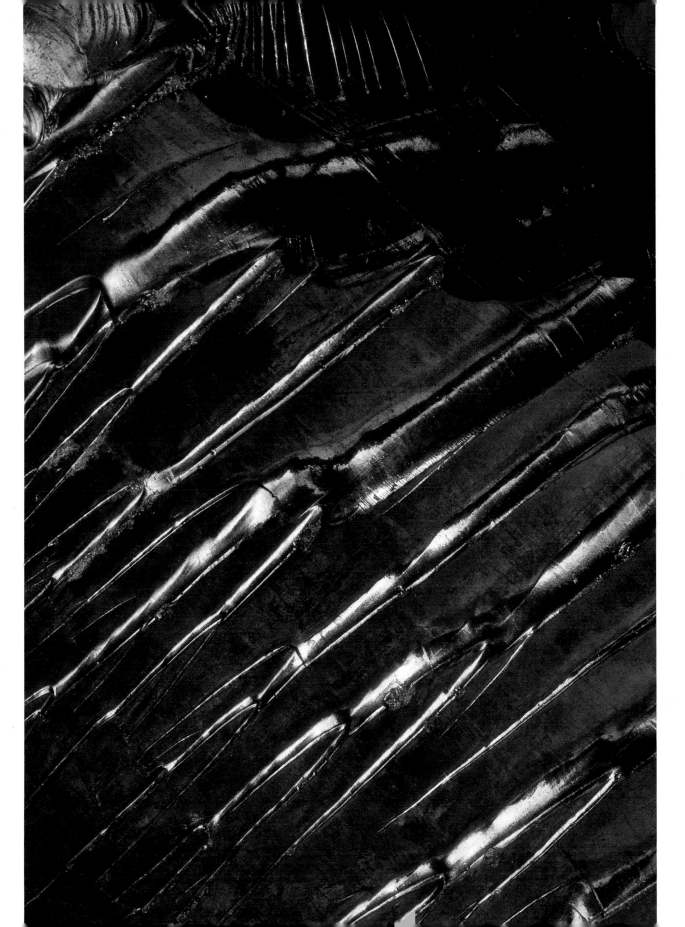

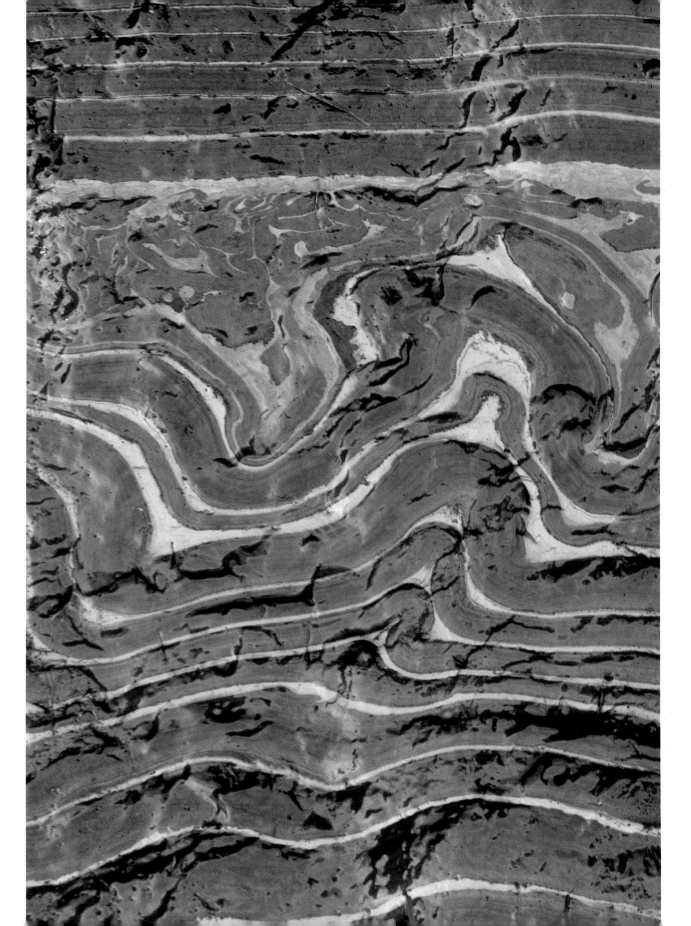

Layers of clay, remnants of an ice-age lake.

Formations of palagonite rock in Kaldidalur, examples of nature's many abstract compositions.

The Eternal Ice

From almost any place on this island the ice of a glacier can be seen shimmering somewhere in the distance. Symbols of intense cold, vestiges of the last ice age, the glaciers have now withdrawn to the highest points in areas with heavy precipitation, yet by human notions of size they are still of giant proportions. It is evident, therefore, that the country bears its name with justification.

Along with the primeval forces of the earth's core, the glaciers have had a determining influence on the topographical features of the island. Wherever they still exist, they continue their ceaseless work: scraping, forming, and wearing away at the surface of the earth.

Whole landscapes lie buried under the mantles of ice, which in places may be up to one kilometre thick. Like monstrous tentacles, the valley glaciers radiate outwards from the central ice mass, leaving deep scars on the sides of mountains as the ice moves down their slopes.

It is a world of paralysing cold, and yet there are farms on the south coast that are less than one kilometre from the frigid tongues of Vatnajökull. This glacier occupies a special position, not only because of its enormous size but also because of the volcanic activity under its western half. The heat from solfataras creates pockets of water inside the ice mass. Occasionally, these deposits of water escape, bursting forth from beneath the glacier and causing floods that are especially spectacular in the outwash plain of Skeidarársandur.

Towering ice wall of a glacial
front (preceding page).

Icebergs floating on the glacial
lagoon at Breidamerkurjökull.

Cones of debris on Skaftárjökull.

Ice cave in Kverkfjöll.

84

Hot springs eat away at the ice of this small glacier at Hrafntinnusker.

The heavily crevassed ablation zone of the Morsár glacier at Skaftafell.

Due to a storm a layer of dust has settled on the ice sheet of lake Kleifarvatn and is illuminated by the low midwinter sun.

Snowdrifts on Hrísey, an island in Eyjafjördur In the dead of winter, the sun barely makes it above the horizon.

The glacier and thermal streams represent the extreme contrasts in the Kaldaklof Mountains.

A melt-water stream meanders through glacial ice.

High above the icy stream of Skaftárjökull.

In the icy clutches of winter Kleifarvatn freezes over.

Evening near Skeidarárjökull. The broad apron of the glacier creeps down into the barren plain of Skeidarársandur, periodically the site of enormous glacial floods.